The Master's Call

Allen W. McDaniel, Jr.

McDaniel, Allen W., Jr.

ISBN 0-9725816-0-X
Christian Living / Inspirational

Printed in the United States

To
Alice
How beautiful is your love, my sister, my bride

Allen W. McDaniel, Jr.

"This time I knew I heard a voice,
A voice so sweet and strange,
A voice that came from everywhere,
A voice that called my name
. . . . .
And I was left to live,
The Master had a reason,
Life is His to take or give.
A miracle performed that night,
I wasn't meant to die."

lyrics from
The Master's Call
sung by
Marty Robbins
from
"Gunfighter's Ballads and Trail Songs"
Columbia Records 1959
#1349

INTRODUCTION

This is not my testimony!

At least, it is certainly not my whole testimony. It is only a small part of what God has done in my life. It is however an important part, and a part that I feel that the Lord has told me to share, that I might proclaim the "great things He has done for me."

There is no place here in the introduction where I, like many authors, acknowledge the part that others have played either in the events detailed herein or in the making of this little book. That is not because there are none, but rather because there are so many. The Lord has placed so many wonderful people in my life, people who have blessed me in so many ways, that it would be impractical to name them all here. But they know who they are, and far more importantly, the Lord knows who they are. It is also because my greatest desire is that the Lord alone receives the Glory!

One thing that I would like to mention has to do with the title of this story. When I was a teenager, seventeen years old and living in New York, a friend of mine had bought a record album, *Gunfighter's Ballads*, and while I was visiting with him one day, played a song titled "The Master's Call" for me. It was a cowboy song, not something that I ever would have normally listened to at that time. It was 1961, and I was "into" the rock and roll music of the day.

This song touched my heart, probably more correct to say that it grabbed my heart, though I certainly didn't show it, and I certainly didn't understand it at the time. I quickly left his house.

The lyrics I heard that day planted a seed that finally bore fruit on another day, years later, when I, like the young man in the song, encountered the risen Savior, Jesus Christ.

I thank the Lord for Marty Robbins preaching the Gospel through that song—The Lord was reaching out to me, seeking me when I certainly wasn't looking for Him.

Chapter One

I hurt! Everything hurt!

I was bleeding internally, and I could feel it. In less than the time that it takes to tell, I took stock of my condition; a diagnosis that would prove remarkably accurate, even more so than one provided later in the local—very third world— hospital. I could not move my right arm. My shoulder was badly bleeding and broken, as were all the ribs on my right side. My right leg lay twisted at an impossible angle with the knee torn apart and my foot pointed towards my head. The pain I felt in my "middle" was a broken hip and a pelvis also broken in a few places. Blood streamed down my face from a wound on my forehead. I instinctively knew that death was only moments away.

A great booming, yet soft and gentle, voice rent the night—although it may have only been heard in the recesses of my heart. More clearly than I had ever heard the voice of God in my years of serving Him in ministry, I heard Him say to me then.

"Do you believe what you have been preaching?"

I knew just what the Lord meant as he spoke to me that night. Although I knew of His power to miraculously heal and I preached it, that was not what He was speaking about. I saw the gift of His sacrifice in my place and I knew that, yes, I believed what I preached! I preached and believed in the amazing grace of God.

As I lay there alongside a dark and desolate road in Central America, broken in body and wracked with pain, I gave serious and grave thought to seeing Him in just a moment. Now, unable to look in any other direction, I stared into the stars with a smile. I would no longer talk about Him, I would now talk to Him face to face. Even as I said, "Yes Lord, I am ready," the voice of God spoke two words to me. "Not now."

From that moment, I knew that I would live to talk about Him some more.

But I still hurt! Everything hurt!

Chapter 2

Darkness fell early and it fell quickly that night, but then it always does in that part of the world.

Sitting at a table on the verandah of the Villa Restaurant in Belize City, my wife Alice and I enjoyed the tropical breeze blowing in off the Caribbean Sea, a welcome respite from the July heat. The food was good, and we were enjoying the company of new friends, George and Georgia Smith. We were discussing the purchase of a parcel of land from them to build a missionary center there in Belize, Central America.

It had been a long day, starting with an early walk in the jungle to greet the dawn in prayer and to watch the wild parrots. There was no running water or electricity in our little camp in the bush, so Alice and I went off to the creek to bathe, an adventure for two people who had grown up in New York City and its suburbs! Going to the creek to get water, to bathe, or when Alice was going to do wash, I carried my machete along to deal with the snakes, scorpions and other jungle critters who might become a little too rambunctious, as well as to slash at the vines and thorn bushes that would block our passage.

We had lived in the bush, near the small village of La Democracia for a little less than a month, having recently arrived to begin our newest Gospel outreach. We bathed quickly, as little silver fish liked to investigate and nibble on us. We were intruders invading their serene habitat.

The sunlight filtered dimly through the leaves of the mahogany, crabbu, and poisonwood trees, and reflected colorfully off the wild orchids. Finished, we made our way up the creek and back to where our little camp was set up. I was awestruck with the beauty of the area. The bugs, however, were truly terrible; little "botlass" drawing blood and leaving a sting that would itch for a week; thick swarms of mosquitoes, at times like clouds, that buzzed incessantly seemed almost inconsequential by comparison. Yet, we were surrounded as never before in our lives by what God had made, rather than by the works of man, and I loved it.

Mark Swiatosz, and Kevin and Polly Boone had made the long and arduous journey with us from Sanford, Florida. We had driven through the torrential downpours of Tropical Storm Allison on the Gulf coast. Flash floods seemed to surround us as we traveled west, striking near Mobile, New Orleans, Baton Rouge, and Houston. Turning south and heading down the length of Mexico and across the Yucatan Peninsula we often encountered roads that ranged from poor to almost non-existent.

They were waiting that morning when we returned to the campsite. The rainy season, lasting eight months of the year, was well under way, and we wanted to accomplish as much as possible during the infrequent dry spells. Kevin and I had been cutting "sticks," small trees, to build a thatch roof hut that would become our communal kitchen when finished. We performed much of this work under the watchful eye of Frank Clark, our nearest neighbor from the village. Frank would tell us in his lilting Creole what trees to use for building so the "wood lice" (jungle termites) would not consume our work in a week; we told Frank about Jesus so he would not be consumed! Mark struggled, digging through the thick, sticky clay and rock, attempting to build a latrine and septic tank from some old fifty-five gallon drums. He would later share with me that this experience helped him to better understand and appreciate David's glorious proclamation;

> *"He also brought me up out of a horrible pit,*
> *out of the miry clay, and set my feet upon a rock,*
> *and established my steps. He has put a new song*
> *in my mouth; praise to our God...[4]"*

It's truly wonderful how the Lord can take the most mundane, unattractive tasks in our lives and give us revelation of His glory that set our spirit soaring.

Polly had not adapted well to the harsh third-world conditions, or to the tropical heat and humidity of the bush. As a result, she and Kevin were making plans to head back to the United States as soon as they could make the necessary arrangements, so the joy of our fellowship was somewhat muted as the work progressed.

Alice and I took our full sized Ford Bronco, and headed off on the thirty-mile journey into Belize City to get some supplies and meet the Smiths for dinner that night. After driving the half-mile or so through the soft ground of the

---

[4] Isaiah 43:21

high bush in four-wheel drive, we hit the dirt road that led up through the village and onto the Western Highway, one of the country's two good roads. Our campsite was about halfway between the country's capital, Belmopan, and Belize City. Belmopan, with a population of about 3,000 people, had been built in the interior in the 1960's after Hurricane Hattie had pushed destructively through the coastal area. Belize City had been the capital, and with a population of 60,000, it was still by far the largest and most important city in the country.

Along the road we stopped to pick up a young man as he "hailed us" for a lift into town. This was one of the things that we enjoyed about driving these roads. The two principal modes of transportation for most people to get from village to village was either the buses, often bright, noisy, crowded with far more people than seats, and their goods (often chickens), but very reliable, or they got about by hitchhiking. We always picked up riders and had the opportunity to share the amazing love of Jesus Christ with them. This day our rider turned out to be a young believer, a Christian who was seeking an answer from the Lord about working in ministry. He told us he had been praying the Lord would send the "right people" to give him a ride. Alice and I encouraged him and prayed with him as we carried him along into the hustle and bustle of Belize City.

Arriving in town that Thursday, we made a stop in the marketplace, greeted by kaleidoscopic flashes of color and a delightful third-world cacophony of sounds as people bargained in rapid British English, Creole, Garifuna and Spanish. Little wooden stalls filled the space in the dim light under the tin roof of the old market by the swing bridge. From a few, the chirps and squeals of live chicks or piglets issued forth. Others overflowed with meats dangling from the rafters, produce brought in from the countryside, fish fresh from the sea, or herbal remedies. There seemed to be a plant or herb for almost every disease, every malady, and every complaint ever heard of, foraged from the pine ridges of northern Belize to the tropical rain forest of the south. It was hard for us to get accustomed to the smell of the meats hanging in the oppressive heat, covered with flies. We were glad to leave and head off along Regent Street to Benny's Supplies where I was able to purchase a length of 4" PVC pipe for Mark's project. After putting the plastic pipe in the Bronco, laying it lengthwise from the dashboard to the rear window between the front seats, Alice and I spent some hours visiting the shops that make up "downtown" Belize City.

Later that evening, our dinner concluded and an agreement reached with the Smiths, we finally got in the Bronco and headed out over the old, narrow, swing bridge. The bridge, turned by hand twice a day to allow the passage of boats, crosses Haulover Creek, which divides the city in half. It may very well be the world's last surviving hand-cranked bridge. From there we worked our way along the canal, little more than an open sewer, and through the maze of downtown streets. Many were so narrow I often felt as though the sideview mirrors would brush the rickety, unpainted wooden buildings. Soon we were on the old Cemetery Road. This road, aptly named inasmuch as it wound through the center of the city's main cemetery, or the "dead center" as it was often called, provided a great view during the day of "wish willies," large iguana-like lizards, sitting on the headstones and basking in the sun.

The road then became the Western Highway, the country's newest and best road. To put things in their proper perspective, I should say that the "newest and best road" was two lanes, with no lights, no shoulders, and absolutely no markings or lines! It wound seventy some-odd miles, twisting out through the hills to the Guatemalan border. At the outskirts of the city, we passed the ever-burning dump, home of some of the city's poorest people. We had been appalled to see people run and fight to be the first to get our garbage when we tossed it there. The thought had often struck me, and saddened me, that we were here to give away our "treasure" — the Gospel, and all too frequently, it seemed that all some people wanted was our garbage.

The rain had finished falling for the day, light for that part of the rainy season. Now the sky glittered with the lights of millions of stars and the moon was bright enough to cast shadows along the way. That highway, without even one gas station along the fifty miles between Belize City and Belmopan, could be a long and lonely stretch during the day, at night it was possible to travel the thirty miles home and not even see another vehicle.

That night as we passed the small, white road-side post marking 11 miles of progress from the city, it was about 9:00. I was tired and looking forward to a good night's sleep. Alice and I both saw a truck alongside the road at the same time, and saw a man waving us down. My first thought was of just how tired I was, and of the bed that waited for me. That was quickly replaced with a thought of why I was here in Central America in the first place, to serve and not be served—to be an ambassador for Jesus Christ. As we came alongside of him, I drew to a stop. It was a Government truck and the driver explained that the electric system had gone dead, just shut down entirely.

I turned the Bronco around, facing back towards the City and pulled off the road, bringing the front of it to face his truck. That way, our jumper cables would reach if needed. Leaving my lights on, and telling Alice to stay in the Bronco, I turned off the engine and climbed out.

I went between the vehicles and began to check under his hood for loose wires as the driver went to the side of his truck to look for something. The stillness and the immense quiet were suddenly broken by the sound of another vehicle approaching from Belize City. It sounded like a large truck and sounded as though it was going very fast. I looked out and along the road, thinking to wave at the oncoming truck to slow it down. As I stared into headlights that were rapidly bearing down on me, I realized they were headed off the road and not turning! I had just that instant to turn and dive toward the bush as this fully loaded semi-trailer smashed into us without ever having put on his brakes.

I felt the impact and started to fly!

Chapter Three

I hurt! Everything hurt!

The Lord had spoken to me there on that lonely road, and now I had an assurance that I would continue to live. It was with great relief that I knew that I was not going to be leaving Alice in that forbidding, far-away place.

The Lord had asked me if I really believed what I preached. In the days and months that have passed since that night, I have many, many times recalled that moment—that question—that voice. I believe in a God who still does miracles, who heals with a touch or with a word. For many years I had hosted a radio show that aired on both religious and secular stations in New York, Florida, and throughout the Caribbean. The show entitled, "Yesterday, Today and Forever" was a platform from which I proclaimed the love and the power of God—through all time. I knew that what Jesus had done as He walked the earth two thousand years ago, He still did today. And yet, as that question reverberated through my being, miraculous healing was not what entered my mind. One word rang out clearly in my spirit — grace. I knew just what the Lord meant as he spoke to me that night. I saw the gift of His sacrifice in my place and I knew that, yes, I believed what I preached! I preached and believed in the amazing grace of God.

Nobody on earth knows my failings, my faults, my sins as well as I myself do. But any thought of myself was pushed aside by thoughts of the love of God, and the gift of life. Staring up at the star filled sky, I thought of a day many years earlier.

September, 1976:

I was sitting alone at the kitchen table in our apartment in New Rochelle, New York. Alice had gone out with her sister. They were making arrangements to get a cake for my 33rd birthday. Only a month or so before, Alice and her sister had gone off to a "prayer meeting" one night and come back all excited and talking about Jesus. This new-found "religion" seemed to consume all of her waking thoughts, and I didn't particularly care for it. At the time I was the president of a small full-service advertising agency, and money was my primary, actually, my only, concern. Being a millionaire at the age of 33 was a goal that I had long ago set, and I thought that things were looking pretty good at the moment. I told Alice emphatically, "This Jesus stuff is all right for you, but I don't want to hear about it." Although I had been raised a Catholic, and had gone through twelve years of parochial grammar school and a small Catholic boy's college preparatory school run by the Irish Christian Brothers, I had rarely if ever given any thought about going to church in many, many years. I gave even less thought to Jesus Christ. I may have used His name often enough, but if I did, it was only as a curse!

I looked up from the coffee that I was drinking, and saw Alice's new Bible on top of the refrigerator. As if drawn by a magnet, I got up and took it in my hands. I sat back down at that table and said, "Jesus, if you are real, I want to know it." I flipped the Bible open at random and stared at the words that jumped off the page and smacked me right in the heart!

To have some idea of the impact of those words I saw on me, I must make a confession to you, the reader. I had an ego—well, most of us do, but—I had a big ego. I felt terribly important, though in retrospect, not with any great reason. I had been fortunate when Alice and I married in 1967 to have an excellent job as a consultant in New York City. We soon purchased a ten room split-level house in the New Jersey suburbs and bought a Corvette and a new Volvo. I think we were the original yuppies. I left that job to start my own company in Florida. We had our ups and downs for sure, but I felt like a real big shot. I was always comparing myself to my contemporaries and thinking how great I was. That is, I felt really important until any time I looked up into a star-filled, clear night sky.

For as long as I can remember, back in my teen years when I was making great plans for my life, when I was an aircrewman flying in the Navy, or starting new companies later on; each and every time that I looked at the moon and stars, I felt so totally insignificant. It would be like a fist gripping my heart! I would think of the light that I was seeing, leaving its source long before I was ever conceived. I thought of those stars that would still be there long after I was gone and forgotten, and I would feel almost crushed. I would feel useless and completely unimportant.

Now, I looked at that Bible and read these words:

*"O Lord our Lord, how excellent is thy name
in all the earth! who has set thy glory above the
heavens....*

*When I consider thy heavens, the work of thy
fingers, the moon and the stars, which thou hast
ordained; What is man, that thou art mindful of
him? And the son of man, that thou visit him?*

*O Lord our Lord, how excellent is thy name in
all the earth!"*

Psalm 8

I knew in that instant that He was not only real, but that
He also knew exactly what was in my heart; He knew my
secret. I began to flip rapidly through the pages of that
Bible, and at every place I stopped each word became a
word spoken into my heart by a God I now knew to be real
and alive. I also knew the reality that He had been dead—
and more importantly, that He had died for me!

I sat there and cried openly for the first time in my adult
life, not really knowing why, and yet I could not stem
the flood of tears. Nor did I want to, as they seemed to
be washing me clean on the inside. I went through every
tissue in that apartment and was well into our supply of
paper towels before Alice returned. When she did, she
found a new me. I could not stop talking about the risen
Jesus whom I had met that day. The Lord who had spoken

to me and said, "You have had your life, now it is mine!" My birthday gift from God—I was born again! I was given a new heart, a fresh start, and a new purpose—to serve the King of Kings. Of course, I later found out that there had been a plot afoot, Alice had been praying over me at night as I slept and her friends from the prayer meeting had been praying for me each time they met.

Back on the road in Belize, Central America, from the moment He said to me, "Not now!" I knew that I would live to talk about Him some more. I called out to Alice, and now I had time to think about other things, including the pain...

I hurt! Everything hurt!

. . . .

(Alice)

As I was sitting in the Bronco I was looking at the front of the truck, a government vehicle, we had stopped to help. I noticed that it had decals of the both the British flag and the Belize flag. I heard the sound of a truck coming down the road and looked up to see headlights. I braced myself thinking that as this truck passed, as fast as it was going, it would make our Bronco rock. I watched the oncoming headlights as they drifted to the left—straight at us and I realized that he was going to hit us. All I could think to do was start saying, "Thank you Jesus, praise you Jesus." The windshield shattered as I watched, I heard the crash but I never felt the impact. I closed my eyes and kept praising the Lord. I opened my eyes a moment later and saw that the Bronco was wrecked all around me. I remember thinking, "This isn't good." It was then that I heard Butch[2] call me. I tried to open the door and couldn't, and had to keep banging on it with my elbow until it gave way. The only injury that I suffered from the accident was a cut on my arm, which left a small scar, from forcing the door open and a lot of minor cuts on my hands from making my way through sawgrass to get to Butch. It wasn't until two days later that I was told the Bronco had traveled quite a distance, over a hundred feet, crossed the highway and turned facing the opposite direction. That was from the force of the impact; and the truck that hit the Bronco had hit Butch first! We also discovered that the PVC pipe, which anybody will tell you cannot bend, bent around me and held me in place so that I didn't exit through the windshield of the Bronco. Praise the Lord; nothing is impossible with Him.

I worked my way through the high bush and sawgrass and found Butch lying head down in a low spot well off

---

2 Allen has been called 'Butch' by family and friends since childhood

the road. His leg, twisted in a grotesque position, and the bloody wound on his head were the first things I noticed. I thought his brains were coming out! Yet, he seemed very calm.

. . . .

When Alice came over to me, the first thing that I noticed was how calm she was. We would later discover that Doris Holcomb, one of the women from the church that I had served as pastor back in Sanford, Florida had been awakened by the Lord in the middle of the night just the night before, had gotten up and was told to pray for Alice to have peace and for her safety!

Jesus' promise that He would give us a peace that passes understanding, and a peace that the world can't give[3], was certainly evident at that deadly site in Belize.

. . . .

(Doris Holcomb)
On this particular night when I was getting ready for bed I felt an unusual heaviness in my spirit, an anticipation of something about to happen, and yet I had no idea of what it might be. I have no trouble getting to sleep at nights and many times when I wake up in the morning I have a

---

3 John 14:27 — Philippians 4:7

sense of God wanting me to pray for people He puts on my mind. Sometimes the Lord tells me just what to pray for those people and other times it's just kind of general.

I remember this night so well. I woke up at about 2:00 a.m. from a deep sleep, suddenly wide awake, and the Lord spoke to me in a most audible voice—a voice that I knew with no uncertainty to be the voice of God—and said, "Pray for Alice!" I said, "Lord, what am I to pray for?" He just kept saying to pray for Alice. After several minutes of me being persistent, wanting to know what to pray for, God said to me, "Pray for Alice's safety and peace." I said, "Lord, what about Butchie?" I knew that they were always together in anything that they did so I didn't understand why He wanted me to just pray for Alice. After asking this question several times, God said to me, "Just pray for Alice, I will take care of Butch." So I began to pray for Alice.

After praying over and over, for Alice to be safe and for her to have peace, I began to pray in the Spirit. I am not sure how long I prayed, but it seemed like a very long time. I knew the Spirit was touching the heart of the Father and finally a calm, a sense of 'being done' washed over me.

The next morning, I told my husband Rick what had taken place that night. We continued to pray every time we thought of Alice, and it was some time before we heard about the accident. We learned that Butch had been hurt really bad, and almost killed. Even though the vehicle that Alice was in was totally destroyed, she was perfectly safe. My mind went back to the many times that I had heard Butch talk about praising the Lord in his sermons even if you were run over by a big Mack truck. All I could think of was to say, Thank you Jesus for taking care of Butch and Alice. Thank you for such special and dedicated servants."

. . . .

The man we had stopped to help, Francisco (who the next day came to visit with me in the hospital and prayed with me to accept the Lord in his life) was walking around dazed, in a state of shock. It appeared that he might have been hit by flying debris, and the blood on his head was evidence that he had a couple of minor head wounds.

The sound of an approaching car drew Alice back to the roadside, and I began to laugh!

Chapter Four

The pain, like an electric shock cutting through my chest, cut short the laugh.

Although the pain was like nothing I had ever experienced before, I lay there and thought to myself, "This is really funny. How many times had I preached it ... now I get to do it."

"It" was to praise the Lord even if you get run over by a speeding truck!

Years ago, we had left the church in New York that I started and pastored for four years in order to travel around the country preaching, starting Bible study groups, and just sharing the love of God with people. It was a very hard decision to make at the time as the folks in that church had become so close to us, and it was a church that was especially known for the love shown there. I felt however that it was what the Lord desired, and so no real decision was necessary except to follow—we went. Alice and I moved from the home we rented onto a bus that I had converted into a motor home. A new phase of our ministry began. Two years "on the road" followed with many exciting events and meeting many great people, from New England to Florida, from New York to California.

We then stopped in Sanford, Florida to start and pastor a new church. One common thread that seemed to flow through all the preaching and teaching that I did in all of that time had to do with praise. In fact, the church was called the House of Praise.

I knew from Scripture that God had formed a people who would declare His praise[4]. He wants us to praise Him, and we should also have the same desire. Our praise for Him should be motivated by who He is, and what He is, rather than by our circumstances.

---

4   Isaiah 43:21

Over and over through the years I had heard myself say while preaching and teaching, "I don't care if when you walk out of here today and you're crossing the street, you get run over by a truck, you need to still praise the Lord." Now, for some reason, I began to think that it was pretty humorous that I had an opportunity to "practice what I preached."

I lay there and through the pain, intermingled with the occasional groan, I began to praise the Lord. I began to worship Him and to proclaim His greatness to any and all who could hear me.

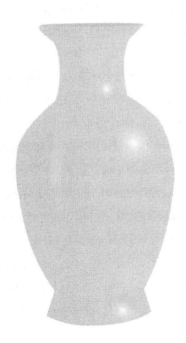

Chapter Five

The driver of the car Alice had heard stopped when he saw the carnage along the road.

Alice quickly told him what had taken place and asked if he would go for help. He said that he would go to the police in Belize City. Before leaving, he discovered that there had been two men in the truck that had hit us — both were dead! Their truck, now terribly twisted and smashed, was loaded with animal feed they had picked up at the city's dock. The two men were Mennonites. Years earlier, a large group of families from this sect had moved into Belize, had cleared thousands of acres of bush, and founded a large farming community. Their community, reached by a means of a small hand-cranked ferry crossing the Belize River, is known as Spanish Lookout. This semi truck, owned by a Mennonite feed company and the men in it would not make it back home tonight!

Alice came back over to me and informed me that the man had gone into the city for help. I was eagerly looking forward to someone showing up who could give me a shot or an aspirin or something to alleviate the pain. I kept thinking to myself that the pain was unbearable. As quickly as that thought entered my mind I would correct myself saying that I was bearing it! Alice said to me a number of times that she couldn't understand why she was not more upset, and would then agree with me that she understood quite well why she had peace—it is a fruit of the Spirit. Throughout the long, long time that we waited for help to show up, my mind would flash to the Bible verse where the Apostle Peter had stated that we are a "peculiar people[5]" and I was in full agreement.

Just before 11:00, a police constable arrived on the scene and informed us that the ambulance was on the way and would be there shortly. When, a few minutes later, the ambulance did in fact pull up, almost a full two hours had passed since the accident. I asked if they could give me anything for the pain and they said they could not.

---

[5] 1 Peter 2:9 (KJV)

Whether that was due to the fact that they had nothing to give me, or due to some policy, I never did discover.

The constable bellowed at the ambulance attendants when, despite my requests, they kept moving me without any support for my leg as they placed me on a canvas stretcher. Their vehicle turned out not to be much of an ambulance at all. It was a small British-built lorry with a small bench along the side of the truck that Alice now occupied. They slid my canvas stretcher onto the metal floor. As the truck made its way along the bumpy road, I was really quite amazed at how much pain I could experience without passing out. I was not sure that it was a blessing. An upright two by four on a wooden stand that must have done duty as an IV holder on other rides toppled a couple of times, threatening to kill me along the way. My lower leg, with the ligaments of my knee torn and the knee bones dislocated, flopped about until Alice got on the floor and supported it. It seemed as though the ride would never end.

Before reaching the hospital, the ambulance stopped to let out a rider they had picked up near the accident site. I wondered how many hitchhikers get rides from ambulances in the United States? At long last, we pulled into the seaside compound of the old, weathered, wood frame hospital. The decrepit state of the hospital did not bother me in the least at that point in time. I figured they would at least have aspirin!

If I expected that I would receive immediate attention due to my condition, I still had much to learn about Belize. Now, I must preface my next comments by saying that in the years that followed, I came to have a real affection for the country of Belize and its people. This was in spite of, not because of, their particular brand of fallen human nature. No better, nor any worse, but so very different than what we were accustomed to. Many of their practices were often frustrating beyond belief to us.

. . . .

(Alice)

When we arrived at the hospital, Butch kept asking them if they could give him anything for the pain. Their terse answer was just a simple, "No" without any explanation or embellishment. They were trying to remove his pants but were having a problem because his leg was bent the wrong way—up towards his head! I hollered at them to just cut the pants off, and finally, agreeing that that would be a good idea, they went off searching for a pair of scissors. I felt like this was an indication that we could have a serious problem here.

. . . .

It was without any derision that we developed our own little vocabulary regarding this "Jewel of the Caribbean."

As the United States is abbreviated U.S., Belize makes use of the letter combination BZ. Their currency, stable over many years by the way at $2.00BZ to $1.00US, came to be called by us BeezeeBucks. In the same way, I always thought of Belize City as BeezeeBurgh; we called the Jeep Scrambler that would later replace the Bronco, our BeezeeBuggy.

The pace at which the medical personnel now attended to my life threatening injuries came to be known by us as the "BeezeeBoogey." To someone from New York City like myself, to whom most of the United States seemed very slow moving, the BeezeeBoogey was the equivalent of moving slow motion through a sea of molasses. I believe it was Winston Churchill who said that getting shot at "without result," was an exhilarating experience. To paraphrase him, getting run over by a truck has a phenomenal ability to better one's prayer life and give it real focus. At this point I was profusely thanking the Lord that He is a "very present help" as it says in Psalm 46, because nobody else seemed to be.

Alice dropped a "shilling," a Belizian quarter, into the pay phone out in the compound, and dialed George Smith, with whom we had dinner earlier that night. George, a native Belizian, worked for the American Embassy, and Alice thought he might know what should be done. Despite the late hour, George and his wife Georgia came to the hospital immediately.

At last, I was wheeled into the operating room. They told me that they were going to reset my knee, pulling it roughly back into position, and place it in a cast. It was a real blessing when the anesthetic sent me off into a place where the pain finally stopped.

Chapter Six

Cats! Big cats, little cats! I knew that I was hallucinating.

I looked around the room, and was reasonably certain that my brain was somewhere other than my body. Another cat walked past the end of the bed that I lay in. I thought to myself, "This is a hospital. There can't be animals wandering all over." The beautiful blue waters of the Caribbean Sea that lay right outside the unglazed windows proved to be the reason. In order to prevent rats from finding their way into the hospital from the seawall, cats were welcomed and encouraged to take up residence within the hospital. While it may not be up to the standards of hygiene employed in most U.S. hospitals, I have to say that it seemed practical, economical, and worked fairly well—I saw no rats.

Paddle fans stirred the air, heavy with heat and humidity, to the consistency of cotton candy. A quick scan of the room showed that three of the seven other beds were also occupied. One fellow, diagonally across the dim room from me, had acid thrown in his face, presumably by an enemy, and was badly burned. Beyond the heavy plaster cast that now encased my right leg, I could see, almost directly across from me, a young man who was at death's door from an appendicitis attack! While rarely more than an inconvenience in the United States, problems like that were often fatal here in Belize. Later, one of my first requests from people in the village would be to conduct a funeral service for a baby girl who had died of dehydration. This young man who now lay dying was from down south in the predominantly Mayan Toledo District, and was considered lucky to have made it to the hospital at all. Later, during his visit at the hospital, Mark spent time that night sharing the Gospel with this man and he accepted the Lord just before he passed away. So far, the accident was worthwhile.

. . . .

(Mark Swiatosz)
Frank Clark was calling out to us, breaking the quiet of the morning and waking Kevin, Polly and me up. He told

us that Butch had been in an accident and was in the hospital. We quickly got ready and headed off into Belize City wondering how bad it was.

We found Butch and Alice in a large room in this hospital that was without any doubt, "third-world." Even though it was obvious that he was badly hurt, Butch encouraged us to trust in the Lord and continue to praise Him. He had heard from the Lord, and he was going to live—in spite of this hospital.

Across the way was a young native guy in one of the beds, a Mayan from down south in the Toledo District, and he was definitely not in good shape. Another young guy was with him, his brother as it turned out, and a Catholic priest giving him the Last Rites!

As the priest left, I drifted over to his bed and I felt as though his painful twisting and turning was not due to the physical pain, but to the spiritual pain of facing death— unprepared. I'm not a preacher, and really felt inadequate to deal with somebody in that state, but I was there, not somebody else. I knew without any doubt that if I asked Butch if he would have been willing to have this terrible accident just so this young guy could hear the Gospel, he would have answered "yes" without hesitating for an instant.

So I just began to tell the two of them about Jesus and how He made a way for us to have eternal life with Him; how the Father had sent Him to die on the cross in our place. I don't know if he was just grabbing at straws or what, but he prayed with me to receive that gift of salvation—and then passed straight into eternity.

The brother broke down, he was as out of place in Belize city as he would have been in New York City, and had no idea of what to do. I helped him with the government and with the undertaker who worked at the hospital to make arrangements to get the body and the brother back home. I hope that he too was touched by the love of God.

. . . .

Alice and I were the only North Americans in the room, most probably the only ones in the hospital, and apparently the only ones to whom the conditions seemed strange. The beds themselves were as diverse as the people who inhabited them. No two were alike, giving the room a rummage sale effect. An old chair sat forlornly at one end of the room, set aside for patients, with a few small, hard wooden benches the only seating available for family and visitors. Unlike the United States, the hospital and nurses there provided only the most basic health care —such things as personal care and food were totally the responsibility of the patient's family or friends.

A nurse came by and clucking, declared her Creole diagnosis of my condition, "Bwoy, ya bruk up fa true." Our best friends, Randy and Ellen Drake, who would play an important part in my return to the States and recovery, and in our future ministry, owned a medical transcription company in central Florida. I wondered how that proclamation would appear in medical records: "Sir, you are really broken up."

Even as she spoke, the pain that I had gladly left behind the night before, tracked me down in that bed and came back to roost! I could move my right arm by using the fingers of my hand to make it crawl around on my chest. I asked her what they were going to do about my broken shoulder, only to be told that it wasn't broken—it was only bruised! I then, in my most officious doctor-like voice, told her what my diagnosis was. She disagreed, and the doctor, one of only two at the hospital, was called. He agreed with the nurse but at my insistence condescended and said that he would have X-rays done. I thought that was a nice idea.

An ancient looking machine was rolled into the room making me think of old Flash Gordon serials and Dr. Zarkoff. They bounced me about on the bed a bit taking some photos, and then declared that I should get up out of the bed—it would be good for me! An attendant and a nurse wrestled me out of the bed and into the only chair in the room. Another medical debate ensued as I tried to explain that whatever I was sitting on (me, not the chair!) was also broken. Seeming to scoff at the idea that getting run over by a speeding semi truck should actually break anything in a human, they finally agreed in any event to return me to the bed. As they were in the process of lifting me off the chair—and a pelvis broken in three places—by wrapping their arms around a chest full of broken ribs, I began to speculate that there was a fiendish plot afoot to finish what the truck had failed to do—kill me. The air burst explosively from my lung as a stabbing pain shot through me. I could not seem to get my breath.

. . . .

(Alice)

The nurse came over to Butch's bed and said that the doctor wanted him out of bed because it wasn't good for him to be laying down for so long, he could get pneumonia. We managed to get him out of bed and put him in a wheel chair. The nurse also gave him a breathing device to use to strengthen his lungs. It was the kind that you blow into and try to move the plastic ball to a certain height.

Well, he suffered through almost an hour in the wheel chair, the whole time Mark and I were trying to get him in a comfortable position. When I finally realized how ridiculous this was I told the nurse that he had to go back to bed because he was in too much pain sitting in the wheel chair. I think that they wanted him to spend two to three hours sitting in the wheelchair because she had mentioned something about him needing to be up longer. I think back to this incident now and shudder and at the same time praise God being able to see how His hand was on Butch, after finding out from the VA hospital in the States the extent of his injuries-broken ribs, broken shoulder, broken pelvis and hip-and here we were shuffling him around like a sack of potatoes. Butch at this point told the nurses that he wanted ten big guys to lift him back into bed because the nurses weren't able to. So she did manage to round up a couple of men, not medical attendants, but visitors of other patients, to help.

The beds in the ward were all different sizes. The bed that Butch was using was very high. The bed next to him was very low so I told the nurse that we wanted to move him into the low bed since they were having a problem getting him into his bed. She said, "No that is not his bed, he must be put back into his bed." She absolutely refused to allow him to switch beds. So one of the men they recruited grabbed Butch around his chest to lift him, Butch has been telling these guys not to touch him around the ribs. Then Butch yelled and hunched over. I was down on the floor holding up his cast to support the weight. It was made out of plaster of Paris so it was extremely heavy. He gasped, "You've punctured my lung." The nurse was standing there and I yelled for her to hurry and get the doctor. She just stood there looking at him and I screamed, "Go get the doctor, they've punctured his lung!"

The doctor came in looked at Butch standing next to his bed hunched over and said, "I can't examine him like that he has to be in his bed." She refused to do anything until he was lying down in the bed.

Somehow they managed to get him in his bed and they brought in a portable x-ray machine to take an x-ray. He was propped up in the bed sitting in an L shape and gasping for air. At this time I received a call from the local airline agent who had been trying to get us a flight out the next morning. She told me that she was unable to book any flight for us until Tuesday or Wednesday. I told her that they had to get him out the next day or they would surely kill him because they had just punctured his lung. I told her that there was no way he was going to stay an extra day. She told me that I would have to speak to a supervisor or director of the airlines to make these arrangements and there was nothing more she could do. I hung up and went and stood next to Butch who could hardly breathe and his color was getting grayer and grayer. I just started to cry and I said, "Oh Jesus please help I don't know what else to do."

It was probably seconds later that I heard singing coming from another part of the hospital. They were singing, "I Hear the Sound of the Army of the Lord." They made their way towards Butch's bed. There was only a small group,

The Ford Bronco taken outside of Belmopan, the capital of
Belize, about two days before the accident

The Ford Bronco just after the accident. Allen was standing in
front of this and the truck hit him first. Alice was inside

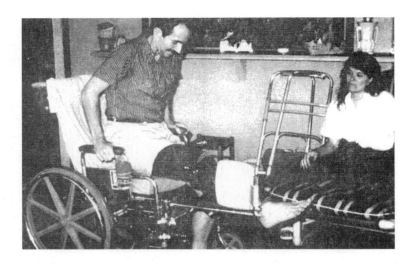

Allen and Alice at Frank and Lee Sorbera's home in New Port Richey, Florida. Then, a couple of months later in Belize

Alice checks for mail at the La Democracia Post Office

The Postmistress, Rachel, seen in the window, had a terrible accident when a bottle blew up in her face and a large piece of glass entered her eye. Alice and I were not in the village at the time and she refused to go to the hospital unless "Mr. Butch" and Alice took her. When we returned later that day, we prayed with her and immediately rushed her off to the hospital. It "just so happened" that there was a doctor visiting that day from Mexico City—and it "just so happened" that he was an eye specialist. He was able to save her eye, and her full sight returned! Need revealed, need met, praise God!

Allen and Alice (and the BZBuggy) returning from the
Mennonite community of Spanish Lookout

Alice shopping in Melchor de Mencos, Guatemala

Allen in front of Frank Clark's home where he, his
wife Myrtle and their ten children lived

Alice and Shakira, Frank Clark's youngest daughter
discussing the glory of the Lord

A small village in the "high bush"

Village women gather at the local "Laundromat"

The hand-cranked swing bridge across the Haulover Creek. The Haulover runs through and divides Belize City.

The Belize River on the way from the City to the airport

A tractor prepares to tow away the truck that
ran off the road and hit us

Mark contemplates his project, building our own little BZCamp
Sanitation Department. Looking at a PVC pipe like the piece that held
Alice in place in the Bronco during the crash

a man with a guitar and two women. They came to the hospital to minister. He was called "Lizzard" and he was the pastor of a small Baptist church in town. They prayed over Butch and shared scripture. Lizard and Butch spoke to each other in scripture. One would say a scripture the other would answer with scripture. I could see Butch getting stronger and his color was returning. By the next morning his lung was completely healed and George Smith and Rudy Boone from the US Embassy had gotten us seats on the 8:00 A.M. Honduran airline's flight out of Belize to Miami.

. . . .

It had been only a few short months ago when I had preached a sermon about sounds that the devil doesn't like to hear. Inspired by the singing of Paul and Silas as they sent forth the praises of God on a night so long ago from a dungeon in Philippi[6], I expounded on how that old devil loves the sounds of human misery—and how those godly men of old failed to oblige him. I used a song that we had sung earlier in that service as a foundation for a part of that sermon. It was entitled, "I hear the sound of the army of the Lord." This song had come to have a very special meaning to me about the power of praise.

---

[6] 1 Peter 2:9 (KJV)

Now, as I lay upon that ragtag bed, fighting for each shallow breath, I heard off in the distance a sound that caught my ear, I heard someone singing, and the words sent a chill through my spirit. "I hear the sound of the army of the Lord. It's a sound of praise, it's a sound of war." A moment later, a man and two women walked through the door. He was strumming a guitar, and the three of them were singing. I forced enough breath out to quote a Scripture verse to him as he came to the foot of the bed and he responded with another verse. As time seemed to stand still, he and I talked, back and forth—using only God's Word. With each Scripture, I felt strength return to my body and I began to breathe easier.

This man, pastor of a small church there in Belize City, was called Lizard. He had come that Sunday to visit with people in the hospital—the Lord had him in just the right place, at just the right time, and singing just the right song. The devil wasn't going to hear any sounds of human misery coming from my bed! I determined that battered body on that battered bed would be an unbroken altar of praise that day!

As this was transpiring in the hospital, Rudy Boone at the American Embassy went to work with the airlines making phone call after phone call, and managed to have Tan Sasha, the Honduran airline, commit to give us space on a flight to Miami early in the following morning.

They would make room for us on the plane, but of course we would have to purchase tickets for seven seats—one for Alice, and six for me!

Visit bibleTalk on the Web for more information and pictures

www.bibletalk.com/masterscall

Chapter Seven

Man becomes frequent flyer in one flight!

I don't know if that would work as a headline in the supermarket tabloids alongside, "Indiana man gives birth to a seven pound watermelon. Martian women named in maternity suit!" (With photos offered as proof right there on the cover). I would, about a year later, convince Tan Sahsa Airlines that their promotion at the time of one free ticket for every six flights to the States should include my six tickets on one flight. But I get ahead of myself here.

Like the little princess in the fairy tale who could feel a pea placed beneath a stack of mattresses, I was able to give a vivid description of even the smallest bump as the vintage "ambulance" carried me out along the Northern Highway toward the airport at Ladyville to the awaiting aircraft. Every movement of that truck was transmitted to my bones, and I don't believe there was a "small" bump—they all came in the large family size. That portion of the Northern Highway between the city and the airport changed in texture almost daily. Road crews battled continually with the ever-shifting base that transformed the road at its best (in the U.S. we'd call that "back-road bad") to its more normal state of something akin to Moonbase 1. This road could sorely test the suspension of the buses, Bedford trucks and Land Rovers that followed its twisting path along the seafront and then beside the beautiful Belize River. The driver of the ambulance truly was concerned for my well being though, and crept along the worst parts of the road.

At the Philip Goldson Airport we bypassed the "International" (and only) Terminal, a small, weather-worn old block building (replaced now by a new facility) and went straight to the waiting plane sitting out on the tarmac. After hurried good-byes and McArthur-like shouts of "I shall return," my litter was carried up the steps and placed along the folded backs of the first six seats in the cabin of the aircraft. The plane quickly began to roll as attendants strapped me down, and in only a moment the nose of the craft lifted towards the sky and pointed north and east bound for the U.S. and medical attention.

Of course, there were a few minor details: I carried no medical insurance, and we weren't sure we actually had anyplace to go once we arrived in Miami!

. . . .

(Ellen Drake)

We were awakened about 2 a.m. by the hated shrill ring of the phone, and I knew instantly that something was wrong. A light sleeper, I was fully alert as Alice told me that Butch had been in a terrible accident. "How bad?" I asked, dreading the answer. The doctors, however, had given Alice little concrete information about Butch's condition, only that he had to have surgery for his "broken" knee and that he had other "minor" injuries. I didn't want to alarm Alice with a narration of how bad medical care probably was down there (she was already seeing it firsthand!) nor with how bad his "minor" injuries could be. I told Alice we would call everyone we knew and get them praying and she should call me back in the morning to bring me up to date. I said something I hoped was encouraging, and we hung up.

My husband Randy had awakened while I was on the phone, and by four o'clock, we had called a half dozen of our friends from the Sanford House of Praise, who had each agreed to call one or two others. We also called the pastor and some friends from Middleburg Presbyterian Church whom I knew would immediately begin to pray. One faithful couple from our congregation, Bruce and Margie, had no phone, so we got in the car and went over, pounding on their door at 4 a.m. During the two hours that had elapsed, even with horror stories of third world medical care swirling in my mind and the uncertainty about the seriousness of Butch's injuries, I felt incredibly at peace. Already the thought had formed (that would be born out later) that God would not have let Butch live had he not had further use for him. We prayed and praised God and sang praise songs with Bruce and Margie until daylight that morning and separated from them confident that God was in control.

It was Friday morning, and we had to get to our office in Orlando. Randy and I owned a medical transcription service (thus my extensive knowledge of medicine) and we could not ignore our clients. Randy took over running the business completely. Most of my time over the next three days was spent receiving updates from Alice and letting our pray-ers know about Butch's condition. When Alice told me that the doctors in Belize had operated on Butch's knee, my heart dropped. I had no confidence at all in their sterile surgical techniques and knew the dangers of infection. Alice did not know the extent of the surgery, but we found out later the doctors had merely set the fracture and had not surgically opened the knee. I knew, however, that we needed to get Butch back to the States for proper medical care and I told Alice so. I suggested she get the embassy to help on her end, and I would see what I could do from Florida.

Where could he go? How could we get him there? I didn't know where to start, whom to call! I called a Dr. Lionel Foncea, one of our clients whom I knew regularly went to Puerto Rico on medical missions. I told him the situation, and he agreed that we should get Butch back to the States. He suggested I call Dr. Robert Bloodwell, who owned and operated an air-ambulance service and who frequently flew missions of mercy. I knew of Dr. Bloodwell from my years working at the hospital. He was a large, gruff, deep-voiced, seemingly emotionless man whose bedside manner I had often suspected. My first conversation with him was not encouraging. He was frank and forthright. He could fly to Belize, he said, but it would cost us a small fortune. If we could get Butch on a commercial flight, it would be less expensive, and Dr. Bloodwell could pick him up in Miami. "Where would he be admitted?" he asked. "I haven't gotten that worked out yet," I replied. "He has no insurance." I had a transcription contract with the largest hospital in our area and I might try to work something out with them. Dr. Bloodwell gruffly told me that in no way was he flying to Miami to pick up a seriously injured man without a hospital to take him to. He asked if Butch were a veteran and suggested I try a VA hospital.

I spent the rest of that Friday getting the necessary information from Alice about Butch's service I.D. numbers, his discharge status and discharge date, and talking with a representative at the VA hospital in Tampa, Florida. I can't remember her name, but even if I did, I would not give it because I'm certain that, as uncooperative as she seemed at times, she really was trying to help and, in the end, I'm certain she broke a few rules on our behalf. It seemed we would be bogged down in bureaucratic red tape for an eternity. With each succeeding phone call, my frustration built, and each time I talked with Alice, the certainty that we needed to get Butch out of Belize grew. By the end of the workday on Friday, nothing had been settled, and I was desperate. I knew it would be next-to-impossible to get anything done on the weekend.

Dr. Bloodwell had given me his nurse's name and a number to reach her over the weekend when I got things worked out. In Belize, with the help of the American Embassy staff, Alice had arranged for Butch to fly out on a commercial flight on Monday. I called the nurse and gave her the information about the flight. Still, however, I had no confirmation from the VA Hospital that they would accept him. (They needed to verify his service records, a process that usually takes several days.) The nurse reminded me that Dr. Bloodwell would not get in the air until a hospital admission was approved. I felt trapped. Over the three days and nights that followed Alice's first call, I hardly slept. I talked with Alice three to four times a day. After each call with Alice, I was on the phone, pleading, cajoling, arguing with bureaucrats. Randy and I prayed continually. Like the woman before the judge in the parable who got what she wanted because of her persistence, I was determined to do the same. When I could, I tried to transcribe, as I was responsible for producing much of our company's transcription.

Monday morning came and still no assurances from the VA Hospital. I talked with Dr. Bloodwell, who again told me he would not take off from Orlando without hospital confirmation. I called the VA representative whom I had been talking with. I told her that Butch's flight would be arriving in Miami and there would be no one there to pick him up. I was desperate. Then God intervened. She finally said that if he showed up on the doorstep of the hospital, they would have to see him in the emergency room whether his admission was approved or not, and if they did not accept him he could be transferred to another hospital by ground ambulance. I was jubilant. I called Dr. Bloodwell's office and spoke to his nurse. "He's already in the air," she told me. I couldn't believe it! Under that gruff, military-severe exterior, he was a softie. I was ecstatic! She would call me, she said, when he picked Butch up. A few hours later, she did. I called a Tampa ground ambulance service the VA representative had suggested and with whom I had already made arrangements and gave them the estimated time of arrival. We quickly left the office in the hands of our staff and raced toward Tampa from Orlando. The trip was ordinarily about a two-hour drive, about the same time the nurse had told me it would take the air ambulance to fly from Miami to Tampa. As we raced toward Tampa as fast as we dared, an especially strong summer thunderstorm rolled in from the gulf. The rain fell in sheets, taxing the windshield wipers. The lightning flashed, brilliantly illuminating the entire sky for several seconds at a time. The thunder rolled ominously. It reminded me of a battlefield scene in a movie. Randy drove. I prayed. For once, I said nothing about his driving. "How can a plane land in all this?" I thought. Would three days of being thwarted at every turn and sudden success founder on this stormy afternoon? I remembered Butch and Alice's frequent admonishment to praise the Lord in all things. I stopped pleading with God and started to praise Him. The storm continued.

We arrived at the airport just as the ambulance sped away and Dr. Bloodwell's plane was taxiing down the runway.

I couldn't believe that they had landed. We hopped back in our car and raced to the VA hospital, arriving only moments after the ambulance. We hugged Alice, were reassured about Butch, and turned to the task of getting the admission papers completed.

. . . .

When we landed at Miami there were three ambulance attendants waiting to take me to another part of the airport where a doctor and air ambulance were waiting for the next leg of the journey.

The men quickly lifted me from the stretcher I was on and placed me on a backboard. Too quickly I thought. This solid piece of wood offered no cushioning, and it amplified each movement they made, ringing pain in my broken bones. Their jarring steps as they practically ran with me through the terminal were a nightmare. But the best was yet to come. I am not quite sure, but I think their names were Moe, Larry and Curly (I know they were hurrying out of concern for me, but haste makes waste). The doors of the elevator slid open as they went dashing towards it and we went into the elevator at speed—and crashed into the far wall. "Oh, oh," said one, "it doesn't fit." Mad dash out of the elevator, now try it head first—funny, the backboard and I still don't fit. They tilt the board at one end, the foot. As I hang there, they decide that doesn't look good. Mad dash out of the elevator, turn around, and back in head high. I think it was at that point I suggested that they just throw me out a window to the street level and be done with it. If as I believe, the Lord has given His angels charge concerning me, then I am sure that they were jumping up and down at this time screaming and hollering at these guys. But in any event, as Nahum said, "God is good" and somehow we made it down in the elevator in time for another mad dash to the ambulance. I told Alice as the vehicle sped off that if, when we reached the air ambulance, they were not willing to take me off the back-board, that we would just check into an airport motel and spend the rest of our lives there. I was not traveling any further on that thing.

When Alice handed the x-rays she was carrying to Dr. Bloodwell, he held them up to the sky and announced, "Well, he has seven broken ribs and a broken shoulder." These are the pictures from the Belize hospital that they placed on a lightbox and said showed that I was bruised! They strapped me into a stretcher on this small twin-engine plane (no back-board, thank you Jesus!) and quickly lifted off for Tampa and the Veterans Hospital.

One of the interesting things about this entire journey, which would not even become a thought in our heads until some time later, was the fact that there is a large

Veterans Hospital right there in Miami. No one I ever talked with had any reason, let alone a good one, why the plans worked out for me to continue on to the VA hospital in Tampa. The Lord's reasons would be apparent as His provisions unfolded.

From where I lay, I could see between the pilot, flying the plane, and Alice seated next to him, out into the clear blue, cloudless sky.

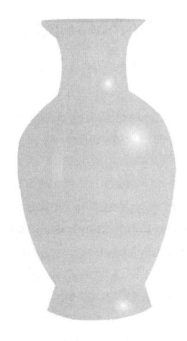

Visit bibleTalk on the Web for more information and pictures
www.bibletalk.com/masterscall

Chapter Eight

Thunder rolled ominously and lightning flashed as the small plane bounced wildly in the unbroken black clouds!

The storm continued to build as we drew closer to Tampa. I had spent many, many hours as an aircrewman flying patrols far into the North Atlantic in the Navy—many, if not most of them in the worst of weather. Nevertheless, I think though that this flight could have made me nervous had it not been for the Lord's assurance a few nights earlier that He yet had plans for me here on earth. A quick little side trip ...

The Apostle Peter wrote, "Whoever speaks, let him speak, as it were, the utterances of God."" When I was first saved, I decided that I wanted the words of my mouth to be His Word as much as I could make it happen. I wanted to respond to things that people said to me scripturally. There is one dear brother in the Lord who would always greet me with the phrase, "What's happening?" I would always respond, "Wars and rumors of wars, famines in diverse places, ..." and to the salutation, "What's up?" I will always tell you, "The Lord! He is high and lifted up, and His train fills the temple." Ask me, "What's new" and I will return Jeremiah's words — "The mercies of the Lord are new day by day."

The reason we have taken this little detour, however, is that so many people greet me with the question, "How are you?" — a question that I will invariably answer with the most wonderful truth, "I am eternal thanks to the work of Jesus Christ." That response has given me the opportunity to share God's love with so many people over the years, and it is a constant reminder to me that what is truly important is not how I may feel at any given moment—feelings that are often changing from moment to moment—but that I have been given life everlasting as the free gift of God.

So now, as the little plane jumped about, not only was I eternal, but also feeling rather immortal in the normal sense of the word. I knew I had a future.

As the plane touched down and taxied to a stop in Tampa I knew that I had a future. But when the ambulance pulled up to the aircraft to transport my broken body to the hospital, I really only had one thought on my mind—would this thing with its emergency lights mounted on the high roof fit through a Burger King drive through lane? I had a future, at least as long as I didn't starve to death. It was now four days since I had eaten and at that time I had very, very little body fat. Now I looked back to the offer of cowfoot soup that I had refused at the Belize hospital with a very different view than at first.

The driver of the ambulance said that he couldn't go to a Burger King because of the incredible rainfall that was taking place, however, looking back, I think that may have just been an excuse used to placate me since he probably thought I was dying. Then as they wheeled me into the emergency room of the James A. Haley Veteran's Medical Center, the first doctor to reach me seemed to concur with the driver. He stated that he had never seen so much trauma in a live human being. I was, as one might imagine, well pleased and encouraged with such "bedside manner." Joined by first one, and then another doctor there was an immediate consensus. One young doctor looked excitedly at me and stated, "This is a miracle!" To which I calmly replied, "I know." He said, "No, no, you don't understand. This is really a miracle!" To which I calmly replied, "I know." At that point he was beginning to get upset with me and might have punched me in the chest or something to make his point that this was really, really a miracle when thankfully both Alice and Ellen spoke up and told him that I was a preacher and was indeed quite sure that a miracle had taken place. I just wasn't surprised that a miracle had taken place. He seemed satisfied with that answer and decided not to beat me into submission. Instead, he had me rushed up to the Intensive Care Unit.

Seven broken ribs, broken shoulder, broken hip, pelvis broken in three places, right knee needed to be opened to determine the extent of the damage-and possibility, if any, to repair it. Internal bleeding had been "miraculously" stopped by a blood clot forced by one of the broken bones. Decades of medical experience between them and they came up with the same diagnosis that I had the previous week lying alongside the road! I was very proud of myself and thought maybe the Lord had saved me that night so I could become a world famous diagnosis guy. But then again, maybe not.

It began to dawn on Alice and me very quickly that we had another situation to deal with, a major one at that. Alice had no place to go and no place to stay. We were told that, unlike Belize, she could not stay there in the hospital. As we discussed this, a visitor showed up. A woman that we had never met before came into the hospital and introduced herself as Sybil Ernst. She was the mother of a member of our congregation back in Sanford who had called her and told her about the accident and us. Sybil lived alone in an apartment less than five minutes from the hospital and told us that Alice was more than welcome to stay with her for as long as necessary while I was in the hospital! We had known both from the Scriptures and from past experience that the Lord will indeed meet all of our needs, but that was to be driven home so much throughout this entire episode. Over and over, need exposed, need met—Praise God!

Speaking of needs, the doctors seemed to be in agreement that I would need a series of operations to repair and rebuild my parts. They were not sure at that point of what would happen with my knee. It would have to be opened and examined to determine the extent of the damage. One thing that they were certain about at that point was that the operations needed on my hip and pelvis were more than they were equipped to handle there at the VA hospital.

Transferred right away to Tampa General Hospital across town, doctors operated on my pelvis and hip and put me back together with wire and pins and screws. The first x-ray that I saw after the hip and pelvis operation put me in mind of a Lionel train set that I had as a child. I was filled with metal. David wrote in Psalm 139 that we are fearfully and wonderfully made, and somehow, I didn't think that the doctors' work-however necessary and well done-was an improvement on the Lord's work.

As the nurses wheeled my stretcher into the room that contained the MRI equipment, I couldn't help but notice the signs all over, and I do mean all over, that warned about bringing metal into this room. The entire machine was one gigantic electro-magnet, and they were about to push a button that would send me along a track and into the belly of this monster. Alice, the nurses, and the operator of the machine had left me and were all in another room with the controls while I was left alone to contemplate my imminent demise, blown apart when they turned on the magnet and the parts inside me became the parts outside me in a bloody explosion. All of God's good work so far would be for nothing, but at least they would have to clean up the mess. (I repent for my desire for revenge) However, due to the type of metal they had used in me—titanium—I did not in fact blow up, which is why I am alive to write this now. Praise God for His goodness. Viewing the results of the MRI, the doctors said that I was about to begin what would be a long path to recovery.

Speaking of needs and speaking of long paths, I was

returned from Tampa General to the VA hospital for knee surgery, where the doctors told me with their best bedside manner that they expected that it would take about a year before I could expect to get about with any degree of normalcy and that it would most likely be many months before I could leave the hospital.

Have questions or comments?
www.bibletalk.com/masterscall

Chapter Nine

I have good news, goodbye!

One month later the doctor stood at the side of my bed and explained to Alice and I that my level of recovery and healing was remarkable. He also said that since, after the operations to my hip, pelvis and knee, I was doing so well—now able to get into a wheelchair—that I could leave the hospital.

But I didn't want to leave! Our home was now in Belize. Our home was in the jungle. You can't get around in a wheel chair in the bush, and I had therapy to go through in Tampa. While Sybil had been so generous to provide a place for Alice over the last month, her home was too small for all of us and certainly not equipped to handle a wheelchair. So now what would we do? We would praise the Lord. So far that had proven to be a good answer. We gave the Lord thanks for whatever answer He would provide and praised Him simply because He is God.

New visitors, Frank and Lee Sorberra, stopped by to see us right at that point. Frank was the brother of a woman, Terry Noschese, who was part of the church that I had served as pastor many years before in New Rochelle, New York. I had met him once before when he attended a bible study I was conducting there. It was a pleasant surprise to see him and to meet his wonderful wife Lena. He told us that they lived just north of Tampa in New Port Richey in a house on the water. They informed us that they had heard about the accident from Terry and they had decided to stop by and visit—and by the way, they were just getting ready to leave to spend two months with their son in Hawaii, so if we needed a place to stay their house was ours!

Need exposed, need met—praise God.

The next few months were a whirlwind, though often in slow motion. Regular trips to the VA hospital for therapy on my knee, progressing from wheelchair to a walker and then onto crutches. Alice and I decided to look for a local church where we could fellowship while staying there in New Port Richey. We went into a Christian bookstore and I asked the young lady behind the counter if she could direct us to a church where "they were excited about Jesus." I recall her words so vividly, "Well, there's a church a few blocks away called Gospel Outreach. I don't go there, but I hear that they're excited about Jesus." So I asked her if her church wasn't excited about the Lord, why bother going? In any event, we visited that local church and shared our testimony, preached, got fed by their preaching, and generally had a wonderful time of fellowship during our stay in town. I went to a gym and worked out with weights and while doctors said that it appeared that my knee would not bend fully again, I would be able to get around okay after a while.

I was comforted then, as I still am today, to remember the words that the Apostle Paul wrote to the church in Philippi, that there is coming a time when,

> *"at the name of Jesus EVERY KNEE SHOULD*
> *BOW, of those who are in heaven, and on earth,*
> *and under the earth, and that every tongue should*
> *confess that Jesus Christ is Lord, to the glory of*
> *God the Father.[8] "*

I am already confessing, and soon my knee will "bow" again. Frank and Lee had returned from Hawaii and we

---

[8] Philippians 2:10-11

found them to be two of the most gracious people that we had ever met. Neither was very tall in stature and Alice and I would often wonder how such big hearts could fit in there. They were truly a gift from God to us. And their pasta was therapeutic for sure!

As the days passed and I progressed from wheelchair to walker, to crutches, to cane. We would sit along the water in the back of their home and watch porpoises swim serenely along the canal just off the Gulf of Mexico and just think about how good God was to us. But my heart longed to be back in the field, back doing the work that the Lord had called us to. When at last at therapy they handed me a cane and took the crutches, we knew that it was surely time to head back to the field for the harvest.

We needed a replacement for the Bronco destroyed in the accident, so Alice and I began to search the classified ads for a vehicle to take us back to Belize.

Need exposed, need met—praise God!

Chapter Ten

As soon as we saw it, we knew that it was the BZBuggy - our BZbuggy.

Alice and I had found the classified advertisement in the St. Petersburg newspaper for a Jeep CJ8 Scrambler. With its four wheel drive, front mounted winch and protective bars around the radiator and lights, it sounded like an ideal vehicle for the rugged, muddy terrain back in our waiting camp in Belize. After a few moments of negotiating with the current owner we struck a deal, and headed off to the motor vehicle bureau to process the paperwork that would make the strong little blue jeep officially ours. One thing that I noticed right away driving was that because I could not yet bend my right knee very well, I had to put the driver's seat back as far as it would go. This created some difficulty for me to push the clutch all the way to the floor. Although it might have looked a little silly, the big wooden blocks that Frank and I put together and taped to the pedals worked just fine, thanks so much. The canvas roof that covered the two seats did not close very tight, but we were certain that in the heat of Central America that would not be such a problem.

Our few possessions packed in the back of the Jeep along with some medical supplies that we had accumulated that would certainly be a great gift for the hospital in Belize City, we said our tearful goodbyes to Frank and Lena and headed off. It was a couple of weeks before Christmas and we decided to visit with the folks from the church in Sanford, Florida and then drive north to New York for a visit with the church that I had started there before heading into Mexico for the long drive down into Central America and back to Belize.

While the fresh breezes that blew through the canvas of the Jeep would certainly be a blessing in the heat, they were a little less welcome as they carried snow into the interior when we reached North Carolina! By the time we had made our way north through Virginia, driving through an immense snowstorm that was dropping significant amounts of snow on the entire eastern half of the United States, we had found that piling some of our clothing around that back vinyl window and turning the heater up all of the way would keep us alive. Arriving in New York, it was wonderful to visit with the church there, particularly as everybody was there for the holidays. Again we were able to testify to the faithfulness of the Lord. We were able to boldly proclaim that what I had once preached in theory, I now preached from experience. While given the choice, I most likely would have not chosen getting run over by a truck as a preferred method of "learning the things of God." However, if it was His choice then it was okay with me.

The day after Christmas, with the snow still falling, we made our farewells and headed south—with the addition of a new blanket to put around the base of the back window and another for our laps. All of the modern conveniences for our Bzbuggy. The snow finally stopped a few days later as we crossed the border into Louisiana, and the temperature began to rise steadily as we headed south from Houston towards the border town of Brownsville. Arriving there, we obtained the papers, insurance and supplies that would carry us through Mexico for the second time now.

Hola! Buenos dias, senor. El Senor Jesuschristo te ama. My Spanish vocabulary now risen to about fifty words, we boldly crossed into Matamoros, Mexico and faced the customs and immigration people.

Chapter Eleven

Por favor. Gracias. Please. Thank you.

It is amazing what power those words have. My attempts at Spanish were heavily peppered with those two phrases, and we found the Mexican people to be as friendly as any place that we had ever been. The farther south we traveled along Highway 180 along the Gulf Coast of Mexico, more often than not well off the beaten tourist trails, the friendlier the people became. In so many of the small villages that we would stop in, nobody spoke any English, or their few words were less than my Spanish.

Prior to leaving the States, people would almost invariably say to us when they found out that we were about to drive the entire length of Mexico, "Aren't you afraid? Don't you know about the banditos? You're going to get killed!" And this from people who continually say, "Yea, though I walk through the valley of the shadow of death, I will fear no evil.[9]"

Yo! I'm from New York City for goodness sakes. Talk about danger. And I had long ago chosen to believe God's Word—we don't travel alone. As King David knew God's presence, we too were comforted.

So, during the next week, we drove down through Tampico, into Tuxpan, down to the lovely coastal city of Veracruz, on south to Villahermosa then east across the Yucatan peninsula to Chetumal. All along the way we stopped and talked with people, gestured and smiled, said please and thanks, pointed to things and said, "Como se dice?" "How do you say....?"

I learned early to say, "Yo soy un predicador." I am a preacher. And then I would ask people to help me preach to them. What a great time we had, and with only the most minor exceptions, what wonderful people. Many people heard the Gospel who really had to work at it with me. As I write this, I am reminded of a later time when Alice and I flew to Houston to meet Randy and Ellen Drake where I

---

[9] Psalm 23

would drive their Izuzu Trooper down through Mexico. By this time I had the trip down pat and actually knew places and people all along the way. Coming across the Yucatan where one can drive miles and miles without coming into a village, I drove around a bend only to be confronted with a line of Federales—Federal Police—blocking the road with machine guns. As we drew to a stop one came to my window and asked if we had any drugs or weapons. I am not sure how many drug dealers or gunrunners actually admit to it, but in any event, the armed men ask—then they search!

I looked right at him and said, "Claro, si!" "Certainly, yes." From the startled look on his face, I don't think he had expected that answer. I hopped out, going to the rear door, saying, "Mira, look. My weapons. La palabra de Dios. The Word of God." And I pulled out one of the boxes of Spanish Bibles that we had loaded into the Trooper for him to open. We spent about forty-five minutes there in the middle of the road with a group of armed soldiers sharing the love of Jesus with them. We drove off with big smiles all around, leaving each of them now with machine gun in one hand and a bible in the other. Our prayers continue for them that they would know which of the two is more powerful.

Now, as Alice and I headed into the seaside town of

Chetumal, our final stop before Belize, we had the growing sensation of "coming home."

This would be our last opportunity to pick up certain supplies that were very hard to obtain in Belize, so we spent the night at a hotel in town enjoying a last taste of air-conditioning for a while.

During that evening, when the heat of the day had given way to the night breezes coming in off the sea and everybody began to stir following the afternoon siesta, the shopkeepers reopened. We strolled through the crowded and colorful shopping centers—the mercados, negotiating for this and for that, a part of the buying process.

In the morning, restocked and refreshed, we started on the last leg of our journey.

Chapter Twelve

"Devil, I'm back!"

People stopped and stared at me. I must have looked a little peculiar to them. As soon as Alice and I had passed through the Mexican border checkpoint, crossed the bridge over the Rio Hondo and moved into the dusty Customs and Immigration compound in Santa Elena, Belize, I stopped the Jeep, got out, lifted my arms in the air and hollered as loud as I could, "Devil, I'm back!"

There is a verse in the Bible that says, "Two are better than one because they have a good return for their labor. For if either of them falls, the one will lift up his companion." The devil may have knocked me down, but the Lord had lifted me up—I had been down, but not out. Now I wanted the devil to know that I was back in the fight there in Belize, and he had better be ready!

As we started the arduous, and generally not very fun, task of taking our belongings, the Jeep, and ourselves through the Customs Office, one of the officers began to talk to me and discovered that I was the "guy who got killed by the truck on the Western Road." In a small country with only limited news service, it seemed as though everybody had heard about my accident. The general consensus had been that I would die once I got back to the States, and if I did happen to live, that I certainly would not come back to Belize. They were apparently wrong on all counts. As that officer called over other people to meet me, this gave me an opportunity back in Belize—the first of many, many opportunities—to share what a great miracle the Lord had performed in my life and how the Lord wanted to work in their lives. I stood in that Government compound and began to proclaim the "great things He had done for me."

Alice and I would find that as a result of this accident so many opportunities to share the Gospel would arise and in so many places that we might otherwise never have been allowed in. Given a choice, I would not have chosen this particular method—getting run over by a truck—to demonstrate the power, faithfulness, and lovingkindness of the Lord, but if it was the way the Lord chose to let it happen, it was fine by me. The prophet Isaiah spoke over twenty-seven hundred years ago and said, "Devise a plan but it will be thwarted; State a proposal, but it will not stand, For God is with us.[10]" I think that the devil had plans for me that night on the Western Highway, but I knew for a fact that God had plans for me since before the foundations of the earth. It is a comfort to know—and to believe—that indeed all things do work for good in your life[11]. This is particularly true when everything works for your good, and for His glory!

When we arrived back in our camp later that day, we were greeted like long lost family in the village. Much of what we had left behind, everything we owned, had been stolen while we were gone. Theft is a very common occurrence in that area. I used to say that throughout most of Belize they practice communism by theft! Now, more graciously, I would just say that they, like the early Church, held all things in common—just not voluntarily.

Through the next year and a half that we spent there, most of the worldly possessions that we had would "pass around the country." We had brought with us some tee shirts bearing the logo of the Christian school that we

---

[10] Isaiah 8:10
[11] Romans 8:28

had started in Florida, the Oak Valley Christian Academy. It was interesting to be walking around in town and see different people wearing those shirts. On one occasion, I was sharing the Gospel with a young man when I looked down and it dawned on me that he was wearing my pants! Fortunately I have the ability to "multi-task." So while I was talking with the man about the Lord, I was talking to the Lord about the man. "Do you see this guy, he's wearing my pants. Why don't you smote him or something." I really wanted him to repent and be saved because I figured the Lord would strike him down on the spot at any minute. Right then, in my mind's eye, I could see a great big grin on the Lord's face. That young man learned something about the Lord that day—and so did I. Fortunately, the Lord had given us a good sense of humor and the loss of my pants didn't cause the loss of my joy—or of my love, the fruit of the Spirit.

After some time, we found it a little too difficult to live in the high bush; me trying to make my way through the deep growth at times, machete in one hand, my cane in the other, trailing vegetation behind from a leg that I could no longer lift quite high enough. Each day's fresh encounters with snakes and scorpions, often waking up with them in our bed, just proving that the Lord does indeed watch over His word to perform it[12]. So we made arrangements to move us

---

12 Jeremiah 1:12 – Luke 10:19 – Mark 16:15-18

and our ministry out of the village. It was the rainy season, and muck, high water, and slippery clay were the order of the day in our camp. Alice said to me, let's stay for another week or so which would have been when the rains started to break as we entered the short dry season. I told her that the Lord had put it on my heart to move *now*, and if it meant getting the entire village out to help pull us through, then that was what we would do! That is indeed what it took, lots of men and women from the village gathered to help us pull our little trailer out through the bush until we hit the higher ground of the little dirt road. We had to leave some incidentals behind, planning to drive back the following morning to gather them. After fond farewells to all of our friends—and now family—in the village, we moved into the relative hustle and bustle of Belize City.

The next morning we left our new temporary quarters at Little Eden in Burrell Boom, the home of some dear American friends, Fred and Sally Kuckow, and drove back to La Democracia to get the things that we had left behind. When we arrived at the village there was a lot of activity, police constables and a couple of guys from the BDF (the Belize Defense Force) were there and seemed quite agitated. It turned out that after we had left, that night, two men had broken out of the prison in Belize City, killed one guard in their escape, and for reasons that were never determined, headed straight for our camp in the bush—the camp that the Lord had laid it upon my heart to get out of right now! We continued to praise Him for His goodness.

During our time there in Belize after that, we conducted a bible study for personnel from the American Embassy and the Lord provided a translator and led us to have a weekly bible study for members of the growing Chinese community in Belize. He opened doors for me to preach at different native churches in the city and to speak at revivals around the area, and perhaps most interesting, to minister to numbers of Mennonites who now opened their doors to us because of the accident and the members of their community who had been involved.

Through some acquaintances in the country's business community I was invited to work with the highest levels of the government to help develop their tourism policy. This placed us in a somewhat unique position as missionaries in that country, where God provided the opportunity for our ministry to reach from the jungle to the city, from the most poverty stricken members of their society living in the streets to the highest executive levels of the government and business community. Our travels took us not only all around the country of Belize, ministering in different cities and villages, but frequently back into Mexico, and west into Guatemala.

We had not been back in the country long at all when, headed to the capital in Belmopan, we were driving out along the Western Highway and just outside of the

City Alice and I rounded a bend and saw a disabled truck just off the road on the opposite side. It's amazing the things that can go through your mind at a time like that—immediately remembering that earlier night of the accident. Nevertheless, I had long ago determined that I would not let my life be affected by fear but that my choice would be faith, so as the two fellows who were with this truck frantically waved at me, I pulled to the side of the road and got out of the Jeep.

I crossed the road and was standing there talking with them when around the bend came a bus—a big bus—going *very* fast. I looked straight at the grill of this behemoth, which now seemed to be bearing down straight at me, and with a real sense of déjà vu, turned and looked up into the tropical sky and said,

"Oh, come on Lord, not again………"

Epilogue

Close enough and fast enough for the air pressure to move me back, the bus went flying by without even touching me.

That moment once again put things in perspective. I would many times later, when faced with the many challenges, and the tribulations that the world and that old devil throws at us, remind myself, "I've been run over by bigger trucks than that!" And He has delivered me from them all.

When, knowing that our time in Belize was done, we moved back to the United States, I began to do something that had long been a love of mine—teaching about Christians and their daily life in the workplace. I conducted (and still do) seminars on biblical principles in the workplace. One of the things that is key, really foundational, to the entire seminar is a concept that I had learned from Scripture and now have had the blessing to fully experience in life. It is this:

The only difference between a problem and an adventure is your attitude!

There is indeed such a thing taught in the Word of God as the "attitude of the righteous" and much of it has to do with the choice you make—or fail to make—to praise God because of who and what He is, regardless of your condition or situation.

I thank God for this particular adventure.....

In His Love

Butch —

Allen W. McDaniel, Jr.

Sing unto the Lord a new song, and His praise from the end of the earth, you who go down to the sea, and all that is in it; the islands, and the inhabitants thereof.

Let the wilderness and the cities lift up their voices, the villages that Kedar inhabits: let the inhabitants of the rock sing, let them shout from the top of the mountains.

Let them give glory unto the Lord, and declare His praise in the islands.

The Lord shall go forth as a mighty man, He shall stir up His zeal like a man of war: He shall cry, yes, roar; He shall prevail against his enemies.

{Isaiah 42:10-13}

These verses from the Prophet Isaiah, twenty-seven hundred years ago reveal an amazing truth; the Lord doesn't really need us to do the battle, we only have to be His cheerleaders.

"Go, God, go!"

About the Author

From the sophistication of Park Avenue in the concrete canyons of New York City, near the Arctic Circle in Iceland, to the steamy bush of the Central American jungle, as well as just about everywhere else in between, he has lived life to the fullest!

After a tour of duty flying as an aircrewman with the U.S Navy that included being a part of the recovery team in NASA's Gemini Space program, Allen worked for a major corporation in New York as a consultant specializing in communications.

He served as the pastor of a church in the suburbs of New York City, and for many years hosted a radio broadcast on both secular and religious stations in New York, Florida, and the Caribbean entitled, "Yesterday, Today and Forever."

In the early 1980's, Allen and his wife Alice traveled across the United States as he preached and taught, and they sang in churches of many denominations. After this they founded a church and school in central Florida. It was from there that they were called to enter the mission field, leaving in 1989 for the Central American bush.

Returning to live in the United States, Allen and Alice began a ministry dedicated to preaching and teaching about the practical application of God's Word in people's everyday life — at home, at work, in every part of life.

Contact Allen by email at: *allenm@bibletalk.com*

Visit Allen at www.bibletalk.com

About the Reader

It may be unusual (at least I certainly hope it is) to be hit by a speeding truck in Central America, and more unusual yet to live through the experience—but there is nothing terribly unusual about somebody needing a touch from the Lord. There is nothing unusual about a person being in a place where it seems as though there is just no answer and no hope in the world, no place to turn. You may even be there now!

There is nothing unusual about Jesus reaching down and intervening, bringing life where you can only imagine death. There is nothing unusual about His voice cutting through the darkness and the pain to bring light; to bring peace and joy in the midst of the pain! In that, there is nothing unique about my story, He has been doing that all through human history.

> *"Therefore the Lord longs to be gracious to you, and therefore He waits on high to have compassion on you."*
> {Isaiah 30:18}

If you need that touch from from the Lord—if you have not asked Him to forgive the failings and the sins of your life and to become the Lord of your life, then do it NOW! There are no guarantees for tomorrow without Him.